To:

_____

From:

_____

Date:

_____

MY BRIGHT STORYTIME BIBLE

MY BRIGHT STORYTIME BIBLE

DAVID C COOK
transforming lives together

MY BRIGHT STORYTIME BIBLE
Published by David C Cook
4050 Lee Vance Drive
Colorado Springs, CO 80918 U.S.A.

Integrity Music Limited, a Division of David C Cook
Brighton, East Sussex BN1 2RE, England

DAVID C COOK®, the graphic circle C logo and related marks are
registered trademarks of David C Cook.

All rights reserved. Except for brief excerpts for review purposes,
no part of this book may be reproduced or used in any form
without written permission from the publisher.

Library of Congress Control Number 2024948929
ISBN 978-0-8307-8946-7
eISBN 978-0-8307-9054-8

English translation edition © 2025 by David C Cook, United States.
All rights reserved.
This English edition published in arrangement with Abba, Bibles USA Inc.

Originally published in Spanish under the title *Biblia para todos los niños*.
Copyright © 2012 by Abba, Bibles USA Inc.

The Team: Laura Derico, Stephanie Bennett, Judy Gillispie,
Caroline Cilento, Karen Sherry
Story writer and chief editor: Joan G. Angurell
Illustrations: Jonatan Mira Bertral
Interior design: Latido Creativo
Cover Design: Brian Mellema

Printed in India
First Edition 2025

1 2 3 4 5 6 7 8 9 10

010625

For *Blanca and Anna,*
Your excitement and smiles as I read
a portion of this wonderful book to you
every night inspired this project.

contents

To Parents 10
To Young Readers 12
Old Testament 14
New Testament 180
God's Plan for Everyone 276

Creation

Adam and Eve

The Story of Noah

The Tower of Babel

The Story of Abraham

Isaac and Rebekah

The Story of Jacob

Joseph the Dreamer

Moses the Leader

Joshua the Courageous Warrior

Ruth and Naomi — Page 120

The Story of David — Page 126

Solomon the Wise King — Page 140

Elijah the Prophet — Page 145

Esther the Courageous Queen — Page 156

Daniel the Servant of God — Page 160

The Story of Jonah — Page 168

The Birth of Jesus — Page 182

The Life of Jesus — Page 194

Jesus and the Cross — Page 246

The Story of the Disciples — Page 258

The Story of Saul — Page 266

To Parents

**The Bible is not just a book.
It's *the* BOOK.**

The Bible was, is, and will always be the most influential book in the history of the world. No other book has made such a huge contribution to art, culture, and society.

The aim of this collection of Bible stories is to explain the main teachings and stories of the Bible to young readers using language they can understand, while remaining faithful to what Scripture says.

Spend time with your child, and read these stories together.

Each story ends with a question. Ask your child the question, and talk about what the story means.

The Bible is the greatest book ever written. It's the book God gave us to explain the story of salvation. God's Word is the light to our paths. We hope His Word shines bright in your child's life!

Joan G. Anyurell

To Young Readers

Do you love adventures?

Well, get ready, because you're about to go on the adventure of a lifetime!

Find out how the world was made. Come face to face with an evil snake. Sail aboard a giant ship full of animals. Enter a land flowing with milk and honey. Hear the stories of pharaohs and princesses. Watch a young shepherd boy fight a horrible giant. Discover the kind acts of wise kings and the mean acts of foolish kings.

Learn about friendship and love. Watch all kinds of different people go on long journeys, battle their enemies, and follow God together.

And meet the most important one of all, Jesus of Nazareth, the Son of God, who came to bring light to the world. Sit beside the manger where He was born. Watch Him grow up. See His kindness and goodness to others. Be amazed by His miracles … and the wonderful stories He told. And discover what He did for *you*.

If you want to go on these adventures, simply turn the pages in this book and jump into these wonderful stories.

OLD TESTAMENT

The Old Testament is the first part of the Bible.

It explains how God created the world and everything in it. He made the sun, the moon, the stars, the ocean, the trees, and all the animals. And guess what! He also created people like you and me.

Did you know that everything He created was perfect? But when people disobeyed God, everything went wrong.

In the stories of the Old Testament, you'll hear about Noah and the Tower of Babel. You'll find out about a young man whose dreams came true. You'll read about a wicked pharaoh and how God used a man named Moses to free His people from slavery. Later, a young shepherd will defeat a terrible giant and become king. You'll see a girl become a queen and save her people.

Keep reading to discover many more exciting stories!

Creation: the First Day
(Genesis 1:1–5)

In the beginning,
everything was dark
and the earth was empty.
But God did
something amazing!
God commanded light
to shine!

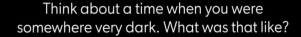

Think about a time when you were
somewhere very dark. What was that like?

On the first day,
God separated light from dark.
He called the light "day."
He called the darkness "night."

The Second Day
(Genesis 1:6–8)

On the second day,
God made the great big sky.

Do you like looking at the sky?
God created it for you!

The Third Day
(Genesis 1:9–13)

On the third day, God created the sea. He made the land, and He commanded trees, grass, and flowers to grow on the land.

Which plants do you like best?

The Fourth Day
(Genesis 1:14–19)

On the fourth day, God made the sun to light the day.

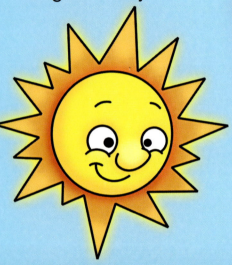

He made the moon and stars to light the night.

At nighttime, count the stars in the sky. How many do you see? God made them all.

The Sixth Day
(Genesis 1:24–31)

On the sixth day, God created the land animals. He made bears, monkeys, giraffes, apes, lizards, and every kind of animal.

Which animal do you like best?

God Creates Man and Woman

Finally, on the sixth day, God created the first man and called him Adam. Then He made the first woman out of Adam's rib and called her Eve.

What do you think Adam and Eve were like?

Adam and Eve
(Genesis 2:1–15)

The Forbidden Tree
(Genesis 2:16–17)

God told Adam, "You may eat fruit from any tree in the garden, except from the tree of the knowledge of good and evil. If you eat from it, you will die."

What did God say not to do?

A Bad Decision
(Genesis 3:6–19)

Adam and Eve disobeyed God. They ate the fruit that God had told them not to eat.

What does it mean to disobey someone?

When God called them, they felt ashamed. They knew they had done something very bad.

Thrown Out of the Garden
(Genesis 3:8–24)

God became very sad.
And because He always acts fairly,
He had to throw Adam and Eve
out of the garden of Eden.
After that, Adam and Eve suffered a lot
because they could not be with God.
But God took care of them.

How do you feel when you disobey?

The Story of Noah
(Genesis 6:1–8)

The people of the earth became very wicked. But one man named Noah was very good.

What are some bad things that people do?

He did not like how people were behaving.
But God had a plan.

A Huge Boat
(Genesis 6:9–16)

What would you do
if God told you to build a big boat?

God told Noah, "Build a big boat. There is going to be a flood." Noah obeyed God. He did what God said to do and built an ark.

Noah finished building the ark.
Then God asked him to take
two of every kind of animal on board.
All the animals came to Noah.

What animals would you want to save from the flood?

The Huge Flood
(Genesis 7:17–18)

What do you think it was like inside the ark?

Once Noah and his family
and two of every kind of animal
were inside the ark, the sky filled with clouds.
Then it rained and poured like never before
and never since.

Water Everywhere!
(Genesis 7:19–24)

It rained so hard, the whole earth flooded.
Only the people in the ark survived.
It rained for 40 days and 40 nights,
but everyone in the ark was safe.

What do you think all the animals did in the ark for 40 days?

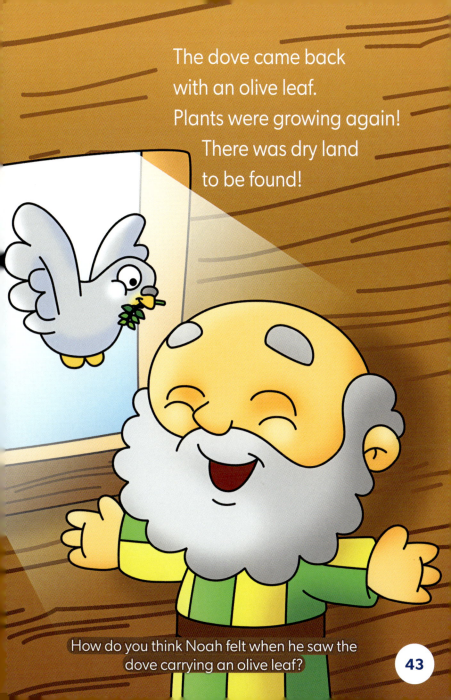

Leaving the Ark *(Genesis 8:15–22; 9:8–17)*

The ark came to rest on a mountain.
Noah and his family and
all the animals left the boat.
Then God promised Noah,
"I will never flood the earth again."
He placed a rainbow in the sky
as a sign of that promise.

Have you ever seen a rainbow?
Every time you see one,
remember the story of Noah!

The Tower of Babel
(Genesis 11:1–8)

Years later, when everyone still spoke the same language, the people wanted to build a tall tower to reach the heavens. They wanted to become famous.

Why did people want to build such a big tower?

Abraham was a good man.
God promised Abraham that his family would have as many people as there are stars in the sky or grains of sand on the beach.

God said, "All nations will be blessed because you obeyed Me."

Try to count grains of sand or dirt.
How hard is it to do?

Abraham Leaves His Land
(Genesis 12:1–5)

God told Abraham to leave his land
because He would take him to a new place.
So Abraham, his wife Sarah, his nephew Lot,
and their servants left their town.
They took with them everything they owned.

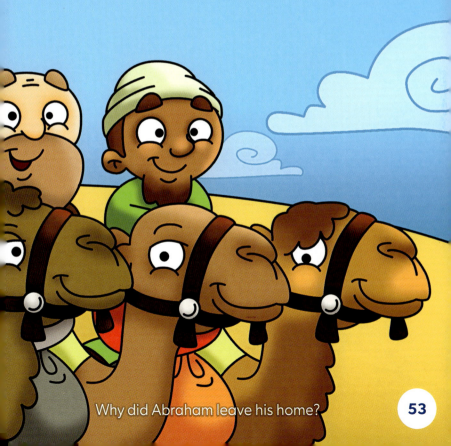

Why did Abraham leave his home?

The Promised Land
(Genesis 13:14–17)

Abraham reached a land called Canaan. God told Abraham, "Walk through the land, for I am giving it to you."

What do you think the land God gave Abraham was like?

Abraham and Lot
(Genesis 13:1–18)

Abraham and his nephew Lot owned many tents and animals. They decided to live apart, so each family would have space and they would not fight.

Have you ever fought with someone? How did you stop?

No Child for Abraham
(Genesis 15:1–3)

Abraham was worried. God had promised him a large family. But he was old and still had no child! He wondered, "Will my servant get all I own when I die?"

What does it mean to keep a promise?

Three Special Visitors
(Genesis 18:1–8)

One day, while Abraham was sitting in his tent, three very special people came to visit him. Abraham gave them something to eat. The visitors had come from God.

Why do you think the three men were special?

The Special News
(Genesis 18:9–15)

One of the men told Abraham,
"Sarah, your wife, is going to have a son."
Sarah was listening and laughed.
After all, she and her husband
were both over
90 years old!

Is anything too hard for God to do?

The Birth of Isaac
(Genesis 21:1–7)

But God's promises always come true. A year later, they had a baby boy and named him Isaac, which means "laughter." God would make Abraham the father of a great nation!

Do you believe that God's promises always come true?

Years later, when Isaac was a grown-up, Abraham sent a servant to find Isaac a wife from among his own people. The servant found a young woman named Rebekah, who watered his camels. She was a helpful woman.

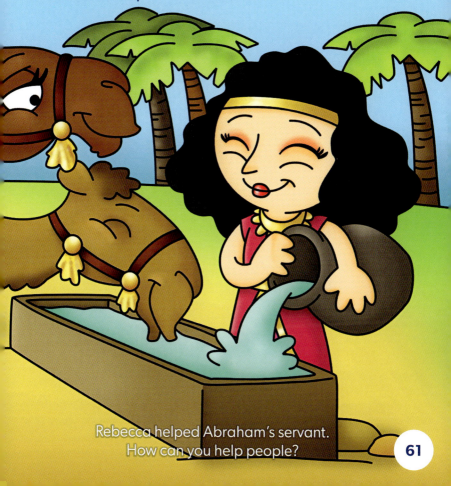

Rebecca helped Abraham's servant. How can you help people?

61

Isaac and Rebekah's Family
(Genesis 25:19–26)

Do you think Rebekah was glad to marry Isaac?

Isaac married Rebekah.
They waited 20 years for a child.
Isaac prayed to God, and God listened.
Rebekah gave birth to twin sons. Esau was born first, and Jacob was born second.

The Story of Jacob
(Genesis 25:27–34)

Years later, Esau went hunting. He was very hungry when he got home. Jacob offered to trade. "I will give you soup, if you give me your rights as the oldest son." Esau was foolish. He took the soup and gave his rights away.

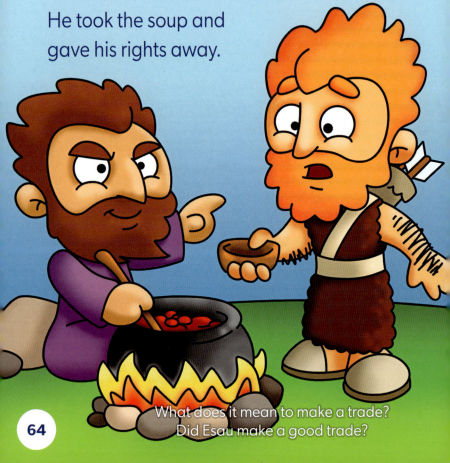

What does it mean to make a trade?
Did Esau make a good trade?

Esau's Big Mistake
(Genesis 27:1–37)

Later, Esau knew he had made a big mistake.
Jacob got everything
that was supposed to belong to Esau!
Jacob even got his father's special blessing.
Esau was so upset that Jacob had to run away.

Why was Esau so upset?

Jacob's Stairway
(Genesis 28:10–18)

Jacob spent several nights sleeping in the desert. He used a stone as a pillow.

One night, he had a dream where he saw angels going up and down a stairway. God told Jacob, "I will be with you and watch over you wherever you go."

Do you feel like God is with you everywhere you go?

Jacob the Wrestler
(Genesis 32)

After some time passed,
Jacob prepared to meet Esau.
Jacob was afraid and
asked God for help.

Why did Jacob want a blessing from God?

A visitor came to Jacob in the night.
He wrestled Jacob until dawn.
Jacob begged the visitor for a blessing.
He realized he had wrestled with God.

Joseph the Dreamer *(Genesis 37:1–8)*

70 — Why do you think Joseph's brothers were angry?

Jacob had 12 sons in all.
He loved Joseph the most.
Joseph had many dreams.
One night, he dreamed that his
brothers were kneeling in front of him.
When he told his brothers about it,
they got very angry.

Joseph's Robe
(Genesis 37:3–4)

One day, Jacob gave his son Joseph a special robe. Joseph's brothers were very jealous. They wanted to know why their dad gave gifts to Joseph but not to any of them.

What does it mean to be jealous?

The Jealous Brothers
(Genesis 37:18–22)

The brothers were so jealous that they thought about killing Joseph. One day, when Joseph came to look for them, they came up with a plan to get rid of him.

Have you ever felt jealous?

The Brothers Sell Joseph
(Genesis 37:21–28)

Joseph's brothers threw him down into an empty well.

Then they sold him to some slave traders who were passing by. The traders took Joseph to Egypt. His brothers tore his special robe and led their father to think that Joseph was eaten by a beast.

How do you think Joseph felt when his brothers sold him?

Potiphar Buys Joseph
(Genesis 39:1–3)

An Egyptian man named Potiphar
bought Joseph to be his slave.
God was with Joseph,
and everything Joseph did was good.

How can you know that God is with you?

Joseph Goes to Jail
(Genesis 39:6–20)

Potiphar put Joseph in charge of everything.
But then Potiphar's wife lied.
She said Joseph had done something bad,
even though he had not.

Potiphar was furious. He sent Joseph to jail. Poor Joseph! He had done nothing wrong.

How does it feel when people tell lies about you?

A Bad Dream
(Genesis 40:1–8, 16–19)

While he was in jail, Joseph helped other prisoners. One was a baker. He dreamed birds came and ate his bread. Joseph explained that it was a bad dream. The dream meant the baker was going to die. The dream came true.

Do you think you should always tell the truth?

A Good Dream
(Genesis 40:9–15)

Pharaoh's top servant, the cupbearer, had a better dream. Joseph told him that he would soon serve Pharaoh again. He also asked the cupbearer to remember him when he was out of jail.

How do you think the servant felt when he heard this?

Pharaoh's Dream
(Genesis 41:1–36)

After some time passed, Pharaoh had a really weird dream. He saw seven thin cows gobble up seven fat cows. No one understood the dream.

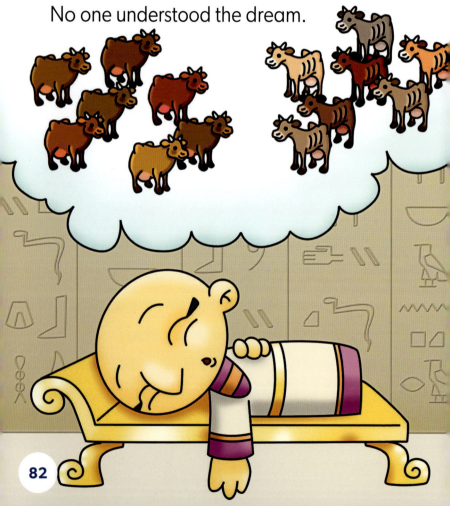

Joseph explained the dream to Pharaoh. He said there would be plenty of food for seven years. Then for seven more years, there would be no food.

Who gave Joseph the power to explain dreams?

Joseph in Command
(Genesis 41:37–57)

Pharaoh saw that God was with Joseph.
He made Joseph his second-in-command.
He gave Joseph a ring and robes
made for kings.

Pharaoh stored food during the seven good years so that Egyptians would not starve during the seven years of no food.

How did God help Joseph?

85

Joseph's Brothers Go to Egypt
(Genesis 42:1–5)

What do you think will happen when Joseph's brothers meet him in Egypt?

Joseph's family lived a long way from Egypt.
They suffered during the years with no food.
Joseph's brothers went all the way
to Pharaoh's kingdom to get food.
Their father, Jacob, waited for them back home.

The Brothers Kneel Before Joseph
(Genesis 42:6–7)

When the brothers reached Egypt, they asked Pharaoh's helper for food.

Why do you think the brothers did not see that it was Joseph?

Pharaoh's helper was Joseph,
the brother they had sold as a slave.
But they did not see him as their brother.
They knelt down before him and
begged him for food.

Joseph Forgives
(Genesis 45:1–8)

When Pharaoh's helper showed who he was, his brothers were surprised. They were also afraid! They thought Joseph would punish them for what they did. But he forgave them.

Have you ever forgiven someone? How did you feel about it?

Joseph and Jacob Meet Again
(Genesis 45:9–28)

Joseph asked his brothers
to bring their father, Jacob, to Egypt,
along with all they owned.
So they did what he asked.
Jacob was so happy to see Joseph!

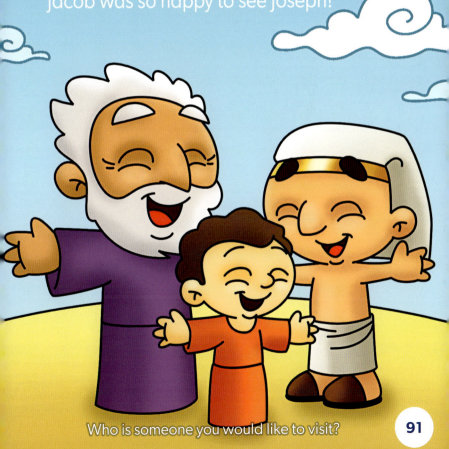

Who is someone you would like to visit?

91

A Cruel Pharaoh
(Exodus 1:8–14)

Long after Joseph died, a wicked king made all the Israelites slaves. He treated them terribly and made them work in horrible conditions.

Why do you think the wicked king treated the Israelites badly?

Moses the Leader

(Exodus 1:22–2:4)

Pharaoh gave an awful command. He said every Israelite baby boy must die. The women who helped with births disobeyed this command.

One Israelite woman had a baby boy.
She wanted to save her baby's life.
She also disobeyed Pharaoh's awful command.
She hid her baby boy in a basket and
placed the basket in the river.

What will happen to the baby?

Baby Moses Is Saved
(Exodus 2:5–10)

The baby in the basket floated down the river.
Pharaoh's daughter saw the baby.
She felt sorry for him and took care of him.
She named the baby Moses.

What would you do if you found a baby in a river?

Moses grew up in the palace. He learned a lot from the best teachers in all of Egypt. But he was an Israelite.

Moses Runs Away
(Exodus 2:11–25)

As Moses grew older, he got angry every time he saw one of Pharaoh's men treating his people badly. One day, he was so angry that he did something very bad to one of Pharaoh's men. Somebody saw Moses do it, so he had to run far away to avoid being sent to prison.

Where would Moses go?

The Burning Bush
(Exodus 3:1–15)

Moses spent a long time in the desert.
One day, he saw flames in a bush.
The bush was on fire, but it did not burn up.
God came to tell Moses to go back to Egypt.
God said, "Tell Pharaoh to set My people free!"

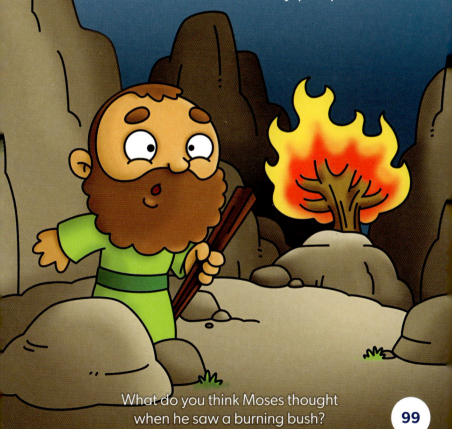

What do you think Moses thought when he saw a burning bush?

Moses and Aaron
(Exodus 5:1–5)

Moses and his brother Aaron went to see Pharaoh. They asked him to let the people of Israel go.

But Pharaoh refused. Moses warned Pharaoh, "If you don't set the Israelites free, some terrible things will happen." But Pharaoh refused to listen.

Why did Pharaoh refuse to listen to Moses and Aaron?

The First Five Plagues
(Exodus 7:14–9:7)

The terrible things, called plagues, started.

First, the river turned to blood.
Next, frogs were everywhere!
After that, gnats bit everyone.
Then a plague of flies came.
Finally, all Egypt's animals in the fields died.
But Pharaoh was so stubborn!

Five More Plagues
(Exodus 9:8–11:10)

God sent more plagues to the Egyptians. First, horrible blisters appeared on their skin. Next, hail fell and hurt people.

Locusts ate their crops, and the sky darkened. The Egyptians could not see anything! But even after all that, Pharaoh still refused to let the Israelites go! The final plague was the worst of all. The oldest son in every Egyptian family died— even Pharaoh's own son!

How many plagues came to Egypt?

105

Moses and all the Israelites left Egypt.
They headed to their own land.
Lots of people went on the journey.
They took their animals with them.
They were so happy to be free!

God kept his promise to the Israelites.
What has God done for you
that makes you happy?

107

Pharaoh's Chariots
(Exodus 14:5–14)

After the Israelites left,
Pharaoh was sorry that he let
Moses and his people go.
He took his best horses and chariots
and chased after them.

With Pharaoh's chariots chasing them, the Israelites reached the Red Sea. The sea was too deep to walk across, and the Egyptian army was behind them. What were the Israelites going to do? They were angry with Moses for getting them stuck there.

Would you have been angry with Moses?

The Waters Part
(Exodus 14:15–31)

God had a perfect plan.
He told Moses to raise his hand
over the Red Sea.

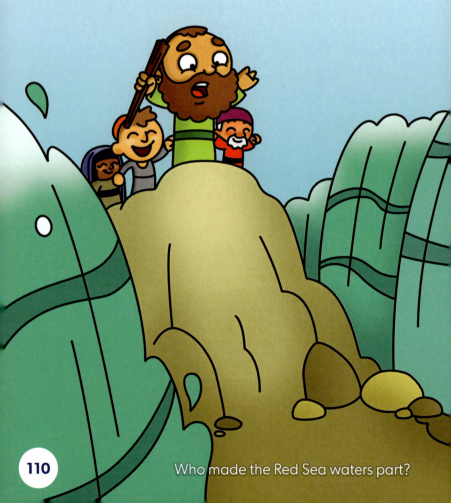

Who made the Red Sea waters part?

At once the waters parted, leaving a path down the middle for the Israelites to pass through. They crossed the sea safely, but when Pharaoh's men followed them, the sea closed in on the Egyptians.

The Ten Commandments
(Exodus 20)

A few days later, God asked Moses to climb a mountain called Sinai. He gave Moses stone tablets engraved with ten commandments.

These were the basic rules that God wanted the people to follow. The rules told how to love God and each other.

Do you know any of the Ten Commandments?

40 Years in the Desert
  (Numbers 14:26–35)

The Israelites disobeyed the commandments. They grumbled against God instead of trusting Him. God punished them by making them wander around the desert for 40 years.

Is grumbling a good thing to do? Why or why not?

Joshua the Courageous Warrior
(Joshua 1:1–9)

When Moses died, Joshua became the new leader of God's people. God asked Joshua to be strong and courageous, and that's just what Joshua did! It was Joshua who led the Israelites into their land. He trusted God and showed great courage at all times.

Joshua and the Israelites moved into the land that God had given them. Many wicked people lived there, but with God's help, the Israelites defeated them. One time, they came to a city called Jericho. The walls were so high, nobody thought they could defeat the city. But Joshua had faith, and God told him what he needed to do to bring down the city walls.

Are you courageous?

Jericho Falls
(Joshua 6:1–27)

God told the people to walk around the walls every day for six days in a row. On the seventh day, they walked around the walls seven times.

Then the priests blasted their trumpets while the people gave a big loud shout. The people did as God had told them, and the walls fell down!
God gave them the victory!

Whose power made the walls fall down?

119

Ruth and Naomi
(Ruth 1)

Naomi was an Israelite woman who lived in a land called Moab.

How can you be a friend who helps others in their hard times?

Both her sons married women from Moab, named Orpah and Ruth. Sadly, Naomi's sons died, so she decided to return to her home country. Orpah decided to stay in Moab. But Ruth said to Naomi, "Wherever you go, I will go too." So Ruth went back to Israel with Naomi.

The Fields of Boaz
(Ruth 2)

Ruth and Naomi were poor, so Ruth went to a field owned by one of Naomi's relatives, a man named Boaz. She picked up scraps of grain that were left there after the harvest. Naomi thought Boaz would make a good husband for Ruth, so she made a plan for them to get married.

How did Ruth help Naomi?
How did Naomi help Ruth?

The Wedding
(Ruth 3–4)

The plan worked!
Boaz and Ruth did get married!
They also had a baby boy named Obed.
Obed grew up and became the grandfather of a great king of Israel—King David.

How did Boaz help Ruth?

The Story of David
(1 Samuel 16:11)

David was a young shepherd who took care of sheep. He was a good shepherd. Whenever a bear or lion came, he would sling stones at them to protect the sheep!

Do you try hard to do your best at whatever you do?

The Future King
(1 Samuel 16:1–13)

One day, a very important man named Samuel, a judge of Israel, visited David's house.

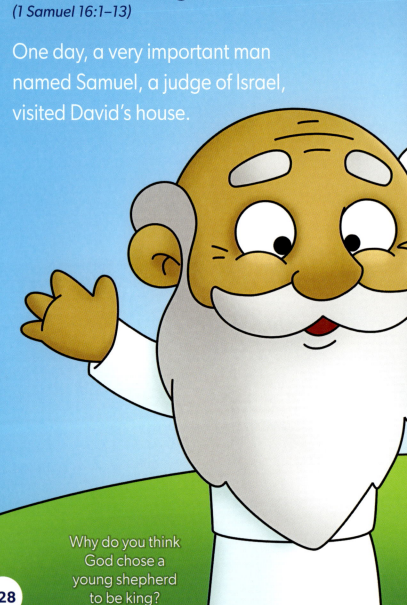

Why do you think God chose a young shepherd to be king?

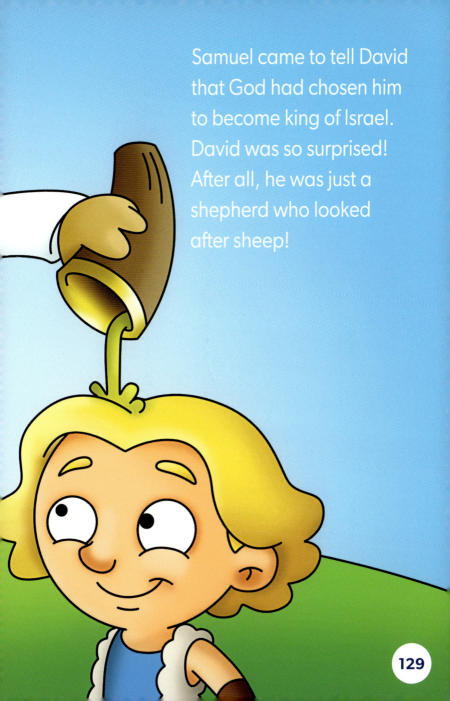

A Scary Giant
(1 Samuel 17:1–24)

At that time, the Israelites had some enemies known as the Philistines. The Philistines waged many wars against the people of Israel.

Their army included a huge, powerful giant named Goliath. The giant was so tall and ferocious that none of the Israelites dared to fight him.

Would you be frightened if a giant wanted to fight you?

David and Goliath
(1 Samuel 17:25–58)

David said, "I will fight the giant." Goliath mocked him. After all, David was just a boy. He didn't have a shield or any weapons. All he had was a few stones and a sling. How could he possibly face the giant?

But God was with David,
and that was all the boy needed.
David took a stone and slung it at Goliath,
hitting him right on the forehead.

The giant fell and died.
David had defeated him with God's help!

Who helped David to be brave and take on Goliath?

David and Saul
(1 Samuel 18–23)

At that time, Israel was ruled by King Saul. David played music to help the king when he felt ill. But King Saul became jealous of David. One day, Saul tried to kill him with a spear.

David had to run away. Saul's men went looking for David day and night, but they could not capture him, because God was protecting him.

Why did Saul try to kill David?

David and Jonathan
(1 Samuel 18:1–4)

Saul had a son named Jonathan, who was close friends with David. Jonathan knew his father wanted to kill David, so he helped him escape.

What would you do to help a friend in need?

137

King David
(2 Samuel 2:1–7; 5:1–5)

How can someone try to please God?

After a while, David became king of Israel. Even though he did some wrong things, he was a great king. In fact, God described David as a man after His own heart. This meant David tried hard to please God.

Solomon the Wise King
(1 Kings 3:4–15)

When David died, his son Solomon became king of Israel. Solomon wanted to be a wise king, so he prayed, "God, please give me wisdom."

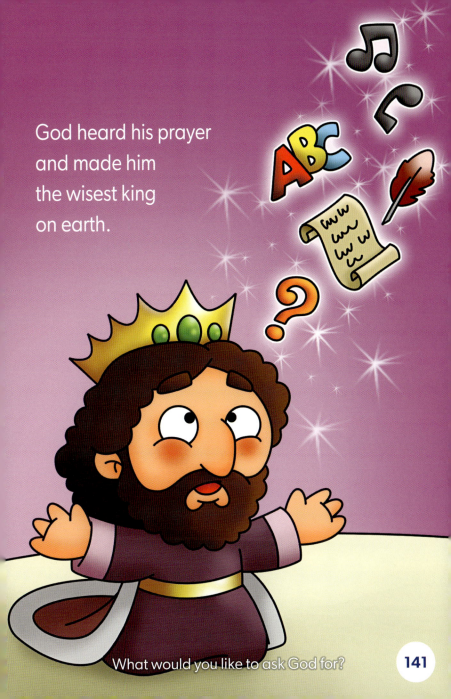

A Wise Test
(1 Kings 3:16–28)

One day, two women came to Solomon.

Both claimed the same baby. To test the women, Solomon said, "Divide the baby. Give half to each woman." The real mother was horrified and shouted, "No! Do not do such a thing! Let the other woman keep him!"

Then Solomon knew she was the real mother. She would rather give up her child than let him be hurt.

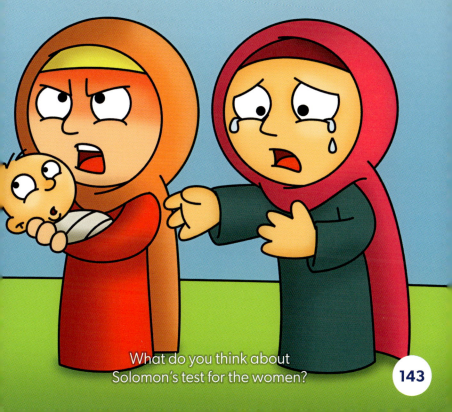

What do you think about Solomon's test for the women?

Ahab and Jezebel
(1 Kings 16:29–33)

When Solomon died, the kingdom of Israel split into two separate kingdoms: one called Judah and one called Israel.

Many years later, a wicked king and queen named Ahab and Jezebel ruled Israel. They did not listen to God.

Did you know that Israel had many bad kings and queens?

Elijah the Prophet
(1 Kings 17:1)

Elijah was a prophet, a messenger for God. He went to King Ahab and told him there would be no rain for a long time.
Ahab was furious.

Why was King Ahab angry about Elijah's news?

Fed by Ravens
(1 Kings 17:3–7)

God told Elijah to go east and hide by a stream. But there was no food there. Do you know who brought food to Elijah? God sent ravens to bring him food.

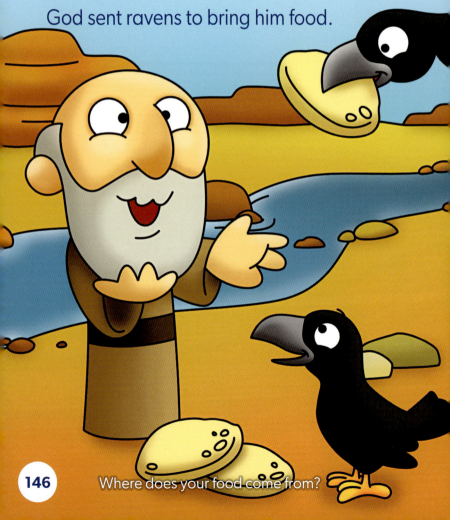

Where does your food come from?

A Widow with Faith
(1 Kings 17:8–15)

Before long, there was no water left in the stream. God told Elijah to travel to see a widow in the homeland of Jezebel. Even though she had very little, this widow gave food and water to Elijah. God gave the widow flour and oil to share for a long time.

God provides for us so we can share with others. What can you share?

147

Fire from the Sky
(1 Kings 18:1–40)

Elijah wanted to show that his God was the only true God. He told all the prophets of other gods to make an altar. Then Elijah built an altar of his own. He said, "Call the gods you follow. I will call my God. The god who sends fire is the true God." The other prophets called and danced, but no fire came.

What amazing things have you heard of that God can do?

Elijah and Elisha
(1 Kings 19:19–21)

Elijah met a farmer named Elisha. Elijah threw his cloak around Elisha. This action showed that Elisha would become Elijah's helper. Elisha gave up his work and followed God's prophet.

Elisha was a helper to Elijah. How can you be a helper?

A Chariot of Fire
(2 Kings 2:1–12)

After a long time, Elijah told Elisha that God would soon take him away. One day, a large chariot and horses of fire pulled the two men apart, and a whirlwind carried Elijah up to heaven.

How do you think Elisha felt when his friend was taken away?

So Much Oil
(2 Kings 4:1–7)

A woman asked Elisha for help. Her husband had died and owed lots of money. Now people wanted to take her sons as slaves, because she could not repay them. God gave the woman enough oil to fill many jars. With so much oil, she could repay everyone and keep her sons safe.

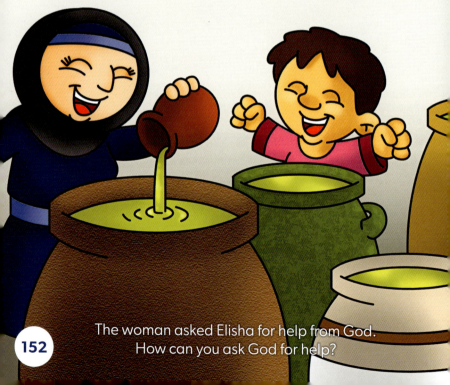

The woman asked Elisha for help from God. How can you ask God for help?

Raised from the Dead
(2 Kings 4:8–37)

Another woman came to Elisha for help when her son died. Elisha prayed next to the child. The little boy sneezed seven times and came back to life. What a great miracle God had done!

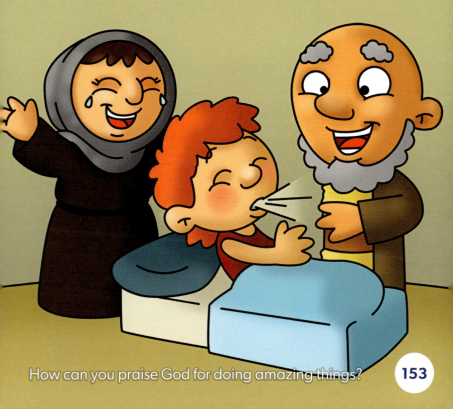

How can you praise God for doing amazing things?

The Healing of Naaman
(2 Kings 5:1–14)

A very important man from Syria was sick with a skin disease. His name was Naaman, and he went to see Elisha to ask the prophet to make him well again.

Elisha told Naaman to wash himself seven times in the Jordan River so that he would be healed. Naaman did not like the idea. But he did what Elisha told him. When he came up out of the river, his skin was completely healed!

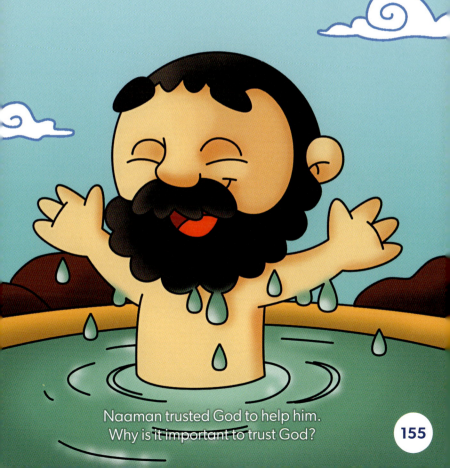

Naaman trusted God to help him. Why is it important to trust God?

Esther the Courageous Queen
(Esther 1–2)

God's people, the Israelites, were captured and taken to the kingdom of Babylon. During this time, a harsh king ruled the land and looked for a new wife. Esther was a young, beautiful Israelite woman. The king decided to marry her, but he did not know she was from Israel.

Who is beautiful to you?

Cruel Haman
(Esther 3)

One of the king's trusted men, named Haman, was extremely cruel. Haman wanted to kill all the Israelites in the entire kingdom. He got the king to agree to his plan.

Haman was powerful. How can power be a bad thing?

157

Esther Helps Her People
(Esther 4–9)

Esther was troubled. She did not want her people to be hurt. But Haman was powerful. Queen Esther fasted and prayed. Then she asked the king for help, even though it was dangerous for her.

Esther begged the king not to kill her people.
The king listened to his courageous queen.
God's people were saved!

Would you have done the same thing as Esther?

Daniel the Servant of God
(Daniel 1)

When God's people were taken to Babylon, a man named Daniel and three of his friends were made servants of the king.

The king offered them foods they had promised not to eat. Daniel and his friends refused the king's food. They kept their promises to God. And they became stronger than all the other servants!

A Fiery Furnace
(Daniel 3)

One day, the king of Babylon made a rule. Everybody had to worship a golden statue. But Daniel's friends refused. They would worship only God. The king was furious and threw them into a furnace with blazing hot fire.

But God sent help in the form of a person, and none of Daniel's three friends burned in the fire. In fact, they were actually walking around inside the furnace without suffering any harm! God saved the men who trusted in Him!

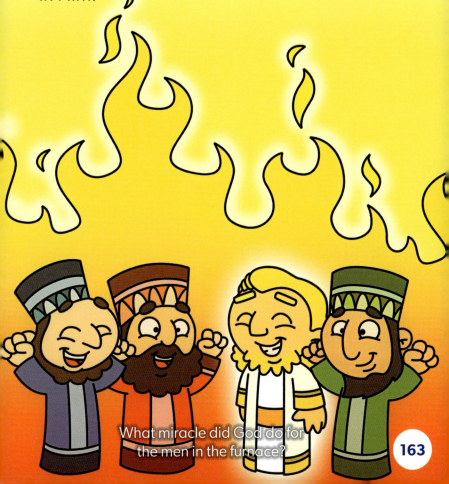

What miracle did God do for the men in the furnace?

Daniel Prayed
(Daniel 6:1–10)

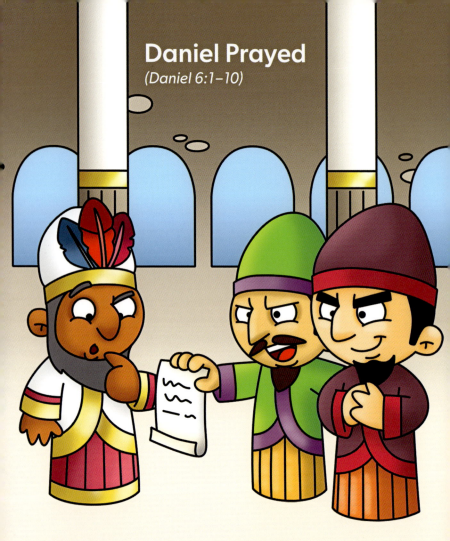

Daniel prayed three times a day. So some men who wanted to get rid of Daniel asked the king to make a rule. The rule said, "Anyone who prays to God will be thrown into the den of lions."

But Daniel knew that God's rules were more important than this rule made by bad men. So he kept praying three times a day. He did not hide his praying. He knew God was more powerful than these men!

Why did Daniel keep praying, even though it was against the law?

Hungry Lions
(Daniel 6:11–28)

Because Daniel broke the law, the king had to throw him into the den of lions. The lions were hungry.

Would you be afraid if you were thrown to hungry lions?

But God sent an angel to be with Daniel. He closed the lions' mouths, and the lions left Daniel alone. God saved Daniel from the terrifying beasts!

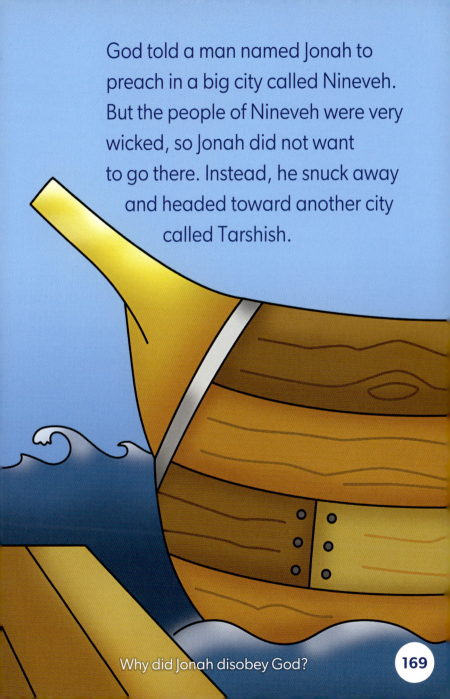

God told a man named Jonah to preach in a big city called Nineveh. But the people of Nineveh were very wicked, so Jonah did not want to go there. Instead, he snuck away and headed toward another city called Tarshish.

Why did Jonah disobey God?

A Strong Storm
(Jonah 1:4–6)

Jonah had disobeyed God. While he was on a boat bound for Tarshish, God sent a huge storm.

The storm was so strong that the sailors were scared to death. Jonah told the crew that he had disobeyed God and that was why God had sent the storm.

What do you feel when you see big storms?

171

All of a sudden the storm calmed down.
The sailors thanked God.
But what would Jonah do in the middle of the sea?

Imagine being in a stormy sea. How big would the waves be?

The Big Fish
(Jonah 1:17)

God sent a big fish to swallow Jonah, and he stayed in its belly for three days and three nights.

What do you think Jonah thought when he saw that fish?

Inside the Big Fish
(Jonah 2:1–10)

While he was inside the big fish, Jonah prayed and thanked God for saving him. He promised to follow God and tell others that God saves us.

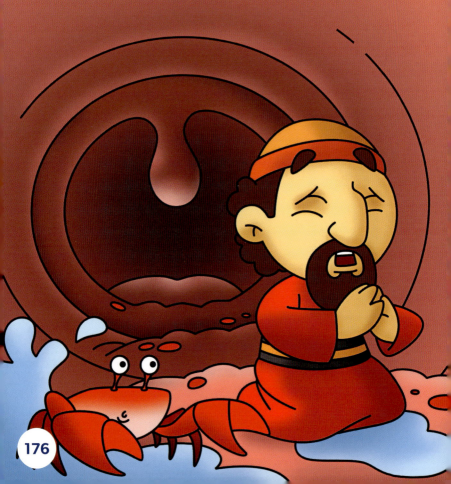

Three days and three nights later, the fish spat Jonah out onto a beach.

When you find yourself in a hard time, do you pray for help from God?

Jonah Preaches in Nineveh
(Jonah 3)

Jonah went to Nineveh, just as God had commanded him. He told the people there to stop doing evil and to follow God. And they did!

What does it mean to obey God?

NEW TESTAMENT

The New Testament is the second part of the Bible.

And do you know what it contains?

The story of the most incredible Man you can know: Jesus of Nazareth.

If you read His story, you will discover the adventures He went on, the miracles He did, the things He taught, and all that He went through to save us.

In the New Testament you will also find the stories of some of the friends of Jesus and how they learned to follow Him. And you can learn how to follow Him too!

The Birth of Jesus
(Luke 1:26–38)

An angel appeared to a young woman from Nazareth named Mary. The angel told her she would give birth to a very special baby: Jesus, the Son of God.

How would you feel if an angel appeared to you?

When Mary was about to have the baby, she and her husband, Joseph, went to Bethlehem. But there was no room for them to stay. What were they going to do? Where would the baby be born?

Where do you think the Son of God was born?

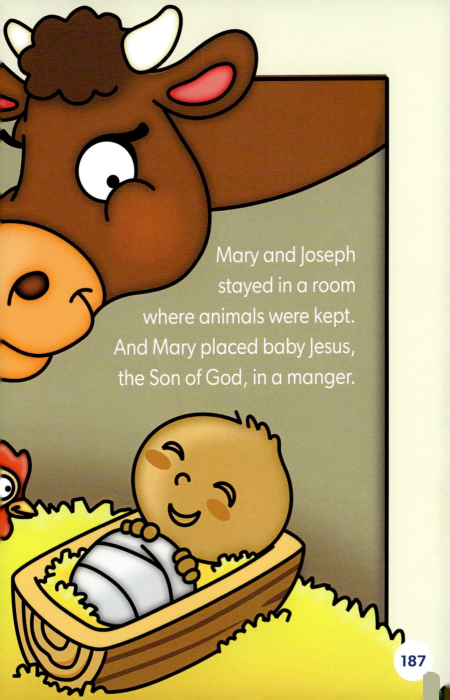

Shepherds and Angels
(Luke 2:8–14)

Near Bethlehem there were some shepherds. When Jesus was born, angels appeared to the shepherds. They were scared.

But the angel said, "Do not be afraid. I bring good news! God's chosen Savior has been born."

Who were the first people to find out that the Savior had been born?

The shepherds saw the baby in the manger. They praised God and told everyone what they had seen.

What would you do if you saw the baby in the manger?

191

Wise Men
(Matthew 2:1–12)

Wise men from the east followed a star to find Jesus. They brought Him gifts of gold, frankincense, and myrrh.

What gifts would you bring to Jesus?

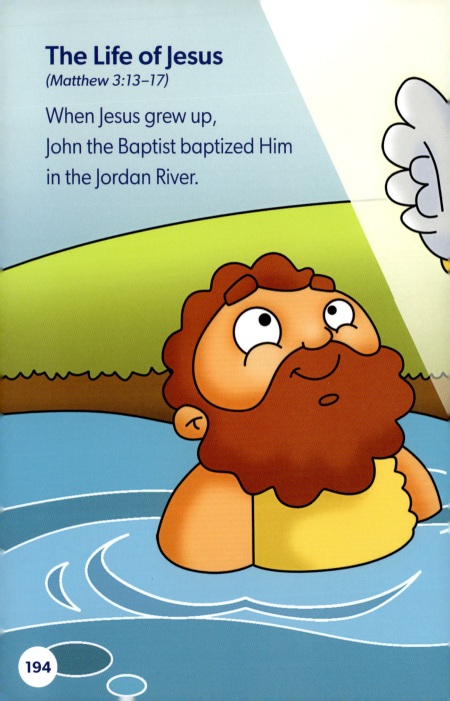

The Life of Jesus
(Matthew 3:13–17)

When Jesus grew up, John the Baptist baptized Him in the Jordan River.

As Jesus was being baptized, the Spirit of God came to Him in the form of a dove, and the voice of God announced: "This is my Son, and I am very pleased with Him."

What does it mean to be baptized?

Jesus Is Tempted
(Matthew 4:1–4)

God led Jesus to the desert.
He stayed there 40 days.
The devil tried to tempt Jesus
with food and power and riches.
But Jesus said, "Get away from me!"

Being tempted means being led to wrong choices. Have you ever been tempted?

The 12 Disciples
(Luke 6:12–16)

Jesus had a lot of work to do, so He found 12 followers to help Him. We call followers of Jesus "disciples." The 12 disciples Jesus called were:

How can you help Jesus, like the disciples did?

199

A Miracle
(John 2:1–12)

Jesus went to a wedding. But the host ran out of drinks for his guests!

What is a miracle?

Oh no! Back then, this was a shameful thing. But Jesus helped the host. He performed a miracle. He turned water into more wedding drinks—enough for everyone!

The Sermon on the Mount
(Matthew 5–7)

Jesus explained many things about God and about how we should behave. One time, many people followed Him to a mountain to listen to His teachings. Those teachings are called the Sermon on the Mount. Jesus taught how to love God and others.

How can you learn about Jesus' teachings?

Jesus and the Centurion
(Matthew 8:5–13)

Have you ever asked God to help someone who was sick?

204

One day, a Roman centurion asked Jesus for help. One of his helpers was very ill. The centurion believed Jesus had power. He said, "If You say the word, my helper will be healed." So Jesus healed the man.

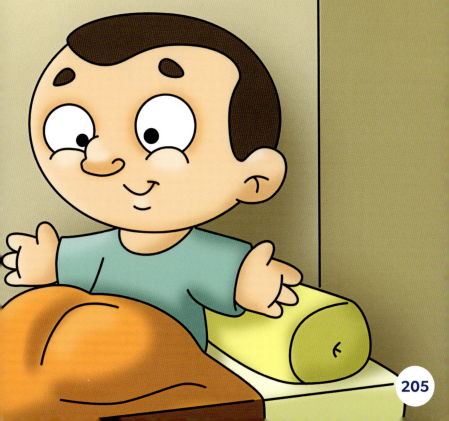

Back to Life
(Mark 5:22–43)

On another day, a very good man named Jairus came to Jesus. He was upset because his daughter was dying.

In fact, she died while they were on the way. But Jesus said, "Believe." He took the girl's hand and said, "Get up!" And she did!

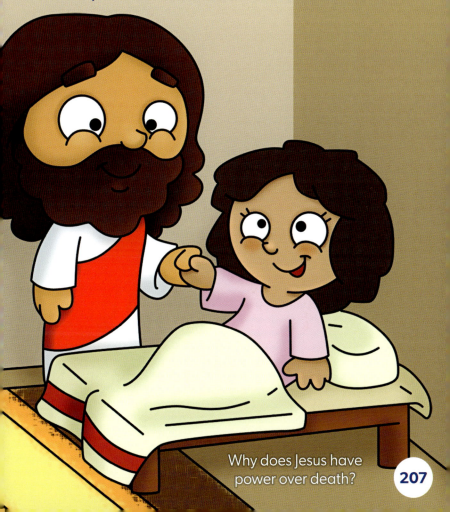

Why does Jesus have power over death?

Good Friends
(Luke 5:17–26)

Jesus healed many people. Once, there was a man who could not walk. His friends took him to Jesus. But there was a big crowd! The good friends lowered him through the roof so Jesus could heal him.

Jesus did heal him! The man walked home praising God!

What would you do for a friend?

One day, the people following Him were hungry, but Jesus and the disciples had nothing to feed them. Then a boy brought two fish and five loaves of bread. Jesus took the food and fed more than 5,000 people! It was a miracle!

Do you think Jesus knows what you need?

Jesus Loves Children
(Luke 18:15–17)

Jesus loved children. He told stories to them and their parents. Jesus said, "Let the little children come to Me. God's kingdom belongs to them."

How can you go to Jesus and be His friend?

The Man in the Tree
(Luke 19:1–10)

Zacchaeus was a tax collector who had stolen from many people.

He was short, so when Jesus passed by, Zacchaeus climbed a tree to see Him. When Jesus saw the man in the tree, He said, "Come down. Let's go to your house!" Zacchaeus wanted to make good choices, so he decided to give back all the money he had stolen—and more!

How does knowing Jesus help people to make good choices?

Jesus and Bartimaeus
(Mark 10:46–52)

Jesus met a man named Bartimaeus, who was blind. Jesus said, "What can I do for you?"

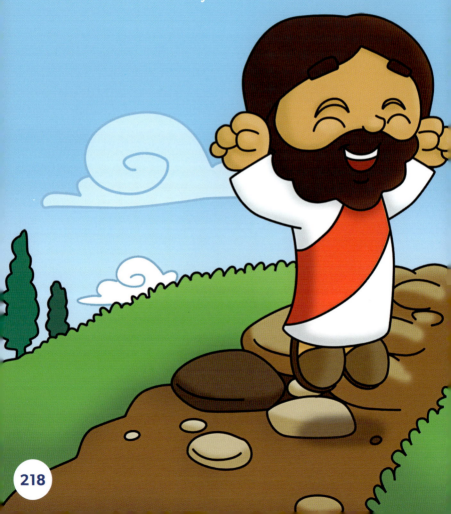

The man replied, "I want to see." So Jesus healed him, and the man followed Jesus.

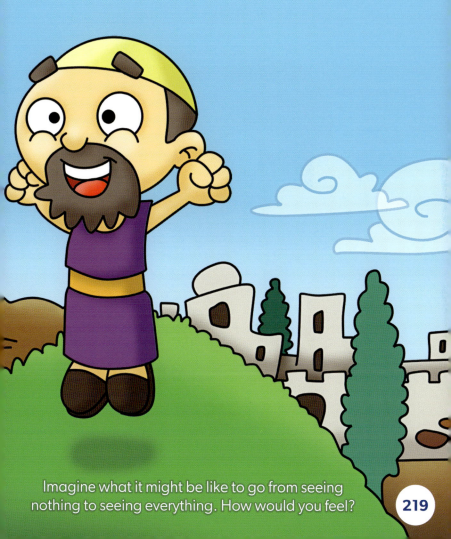

Imagine what it might be like to go from seeing nothing to seeing everything. How would you feel?

The Lost Sheep
(Luke 15:3–7)

Jesus told the story of a shepherd who left 99 sheep to go look for one lost sheep. Jesus is like that good shepherd. He cares about you and will always look for you. He is happy when you come back to Him.

Do you know how much Jesus loves you?

The Lost Son
(Luke 15:11–13)

Jesus told another story.
A young man asked his father
for his share of his inheritance.

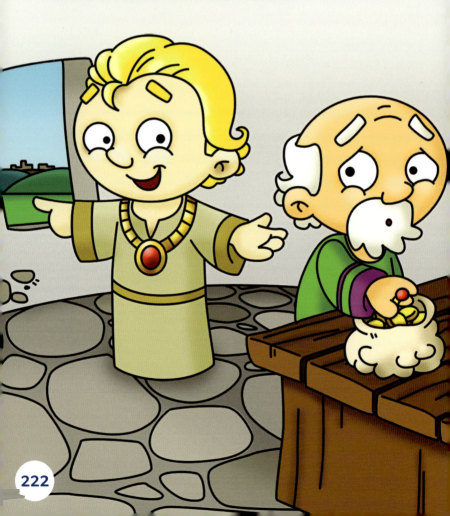

He went far away from home and wasted all the money on bad things. He made many bad choices.

Why is it important to make good choices?

The Lost Son Returns
(Luke 15:14–32)

The son ran out of money and ended up alone.
He got a job feeding pigs.
That was the worst possible job!

He decided to go back to his father's house. He thought maybe his father would let him live there as a servant. But when the father saw his son returning home, he was not angry.

He ran and hugged his son and threw a big party to celebrate.

How is God like the father in this story?

Jesus had a friend named Lazarus,
who became very sick and died.
Jesus loved Lazarus so much.
He cried when Lazarus died.
But then Jesus went to His friend's tomb
and brought him back to life!

Do you cry when you are sad?

Ten Men Ask for Help
(Luke 17:11–14)

Jesus performed many miracles and healed many people.

228

Ten men with a very serious disease called leprosy asked Jesus to make them better. Jesus told them, "Go show yourselves to the priests."

What is one way you can help a sick friend?

One Thankful Man
(Luke 17:15–19)

All the men were healed before they even got to the priests.

But only one of them went back to thank Jesus. He praised God for making him well.

How can you thank Jesus for what He does for you?

A Trap for Jesus
(Luke 20:19–26)

At that time, some jealous leaders tried to catch Jesus doing something wrong. They sent spies to ask, "Teacher, should we pay taxes to Roman rulers?"

They hoped Jesus would order them not to pay taxes but to give only to God. But Jesus looked at a coin and said, "Give to the rulers what belongs to the rulers. And give to God what belongs to God."

What belongs to God?

During the Passover festival, Jesus rode into Jerusalem on a donkey. The people greeted Him with palm branches and by spreading their cloaks on the road before Him. The crowd shouted, "Blessed is the King who comes in God's name!"

Why did the people treat Jesus like a king?

Jesus Washes Feet
(John 13:1–17)

How can you help and serve your friends?

Jesus taught His disciples that everyone who follows God must help others. He helped His disciples by washing their feet. He showed them that nobody is more important than anybody else.

The Last Supper
(Matthew 26:26–29; 1 Corinthians 11:23–25)

Jesus met with His 12 disciples and shared a Passover meal with them.

Jesus knew that very soon He was going to be taken away. He said, "This bread and drink are like Me. I give them all to you." He wanted them to remember Him and His promise to forgive their sins.

Why should we always remember Jesus?

239

Jesus Asks for Help
(Mark 14:32–42)

After the meal, Jesus and three of his disciples went to a garden called Gethsemane. Jesus became very sad. He knew He was going to suffer.

He asked His Father God for help to take away the suffering, if possible. Jesus asked the three disciples to pray with Him too, but they fell asleep.

When you are very sad, who do you ask for help?

Judas Betrays Jesus
(Matthew 26:45–56)

After Jesus prayed, a large crowd came with swords and clubs. They were led by Judas, who was one of the disciples.

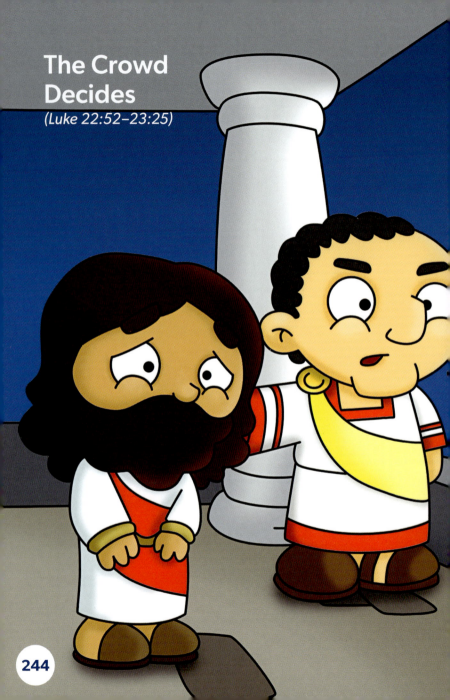

Jesus was arrested and taken to the house of the Roman governor, Pilate. Although Pilate believed Jesus had done nothing wrong, he let the people in the crowd decide whether Jesus should be punished or not. And the crowd called for Jesus to be killed on a cross!

Why do you think the crowd called for Jesus to die?

The soldiers hit Jesus and placed a crown of thorns on His head and mocked Him. They nailed Him to a cross and put two criminals on crosses next to Him.
Jesus suffered and then died on that horrible cross. He was the Son of God, and He died for our sins.

How do you think Jesus' friends felt when He died?

In the Tomb
(Luke 23:50–56)

A good man named Joseph allowed Jesus to be placed in an empty tomb that he owned.

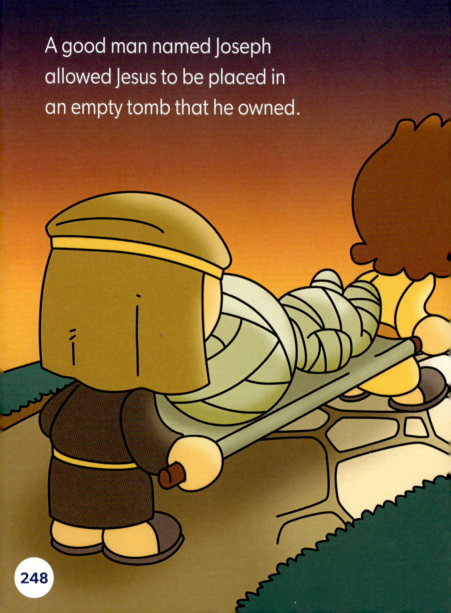

He wrapped up the body in cloth and placed it in the tomb.
Some women who followed Jesus saw His body in the tomb too.
They thought He was dead forever.

A huge stone closed the entrance to the tomb.
Why do you think that was done?

249

Jesus Rises Again!
(Luke 24:1–8)

On the third day, Jesus rose again. The stone that had sealed the tomb rolled away, and the tomb was empty. Jesus had beaten death!

Why is it important that Jesus rose again?

251

Jesus Is Alive!
(Matthew 28:1–10)

On the first day of the week, two women named Mary went to visit the tomb where Jesus was.

Jesus Appears
(Luke 24:33–49)

One night when the disciples were meeting together, Jesus appeared to them.

Jesus proved to them that it was really Him by showing them the wounds in His hands and feet. The women had told the truth! Jesus had risen from the dead.

How do you think the disciples felt when they saw Jesus again?

Jesus Returns to Heaven
(Luke 24:45–53)

After appearing to the disciples, Jesus told them He had to return to His Father. The disciples watched in awe as Jesus returned to heaven. He also told them not to be sad, because very soon they would receive the Holy Spirit.

Is Jesus alive today?

The Story of the Disciples
(Acts 2:1–4)

Soon after Jesus returned to heaven, His friends were meeting in a house when suddenly they heard a rushing wind. What looked like flames appeared on their heads. God's Spirit had come to them, just as Jesus had promised.

Can the Holy Spirit come to anyone?

259

The Disciples Speak
(Acts 2:4–42)

After the Holy Spirit came, the disciples all started speaking different languages. There were people from many parts of the world in Jerusalem, and they spoke many languages.

But when the disciples preached, everyone understood, wherever they were from and whatever language they spoke.
What a wonderful miracle!

What languages would you like to speak?

The First Believers
(Acts 4:32–37)

Many people believed that
Jesus was the Son of God
and the Savior of the world.
They met in homes together,
and they shared
everything they had.

What can you share?

Stephen Sees Jesus
(Acts 7)

One of the people who believed in Jesus was named Stephen.

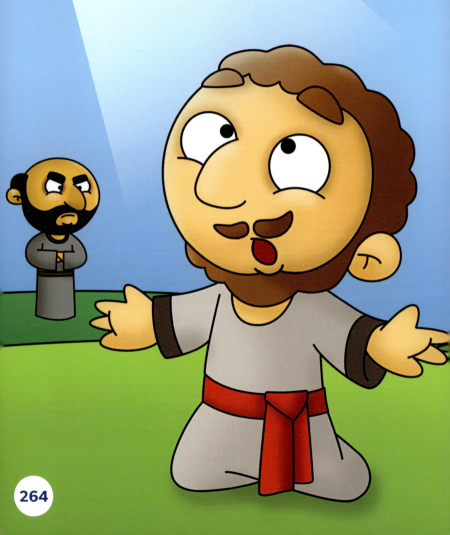

Stephen was a very good man, but many people really hated what he preached about Jesus. So they killed him by throwing stones at him. Just before Stephen died, he saw Jesus waiting for him in heaven.

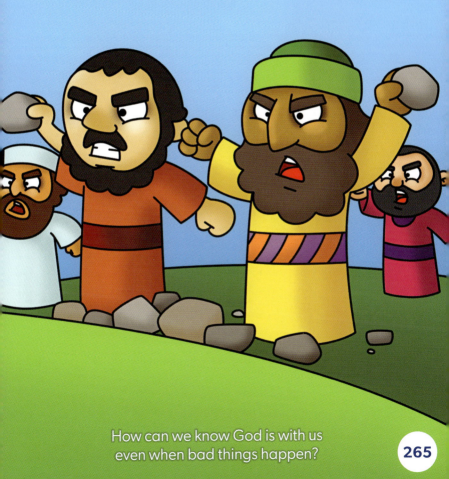

How can we know God is with us even when bad things happen?

265

The Story of Saul

(Acts 9:1–31)

266

A man named Saul did not believe Jesus was God's Son. He was mean to those who followed Jesus. He put them in prison. One day, Jesus appeared to Saul in a bright light on the road to Damascus. He said, "Saul, why are you hurting Me?" Then Saul knew that Jesus was the Son of God.

He was sorry for what he had done and decided to serve Jesus with all his strength.

Why did Jesus appear to Saul?

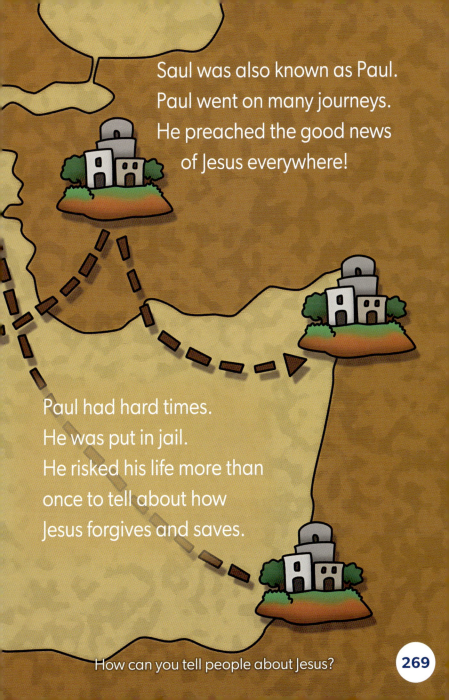

Paul's Letters

Even as a prisoner, Paul wrote many letters explaining what God is like, what Jesus did for us, and how we should behave when we believe in Him. You can read those letters in the Bible, the most wonderful book ever written.

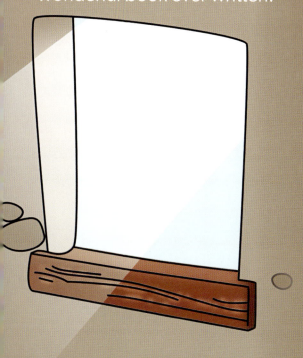

Why did Paul write letters?

Every Day with God

Have you enjoyed this adventure through the book that God wrote for all of us?

Remember that all the stories you've read are true. And you can learn so many lessons from these stories and apply them to your life.

God wants you to read the Bible every day, because that's how He brings light to your life. You can listen to the stories or read them yourself. Not only will you enjoy them, but you'll also learn more about God and what He wants for you.

It's also important to pray every day. Give thanks to God for everything He gives you, and ask Him for everything you need. God loves to hear you, and He loves it when you tell Him about things in your life.

Remember Jesus loves you every day. His story is written in the Bible so we can know how much He loves us. God sent Jesus to die for us and to forgive us for our sins.

Jesus took the punishment for all the bad things we do.

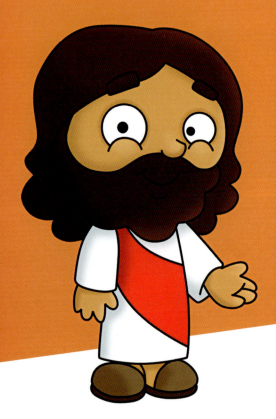

He brought light to the darkness of the world.
And He rose again to shine bright forever!
That's the good news of the Bible.
 It's an incredible story that lights up our world.

We hope *My Bright Storytime Bible* helps you shine for Jesus!

God's Plan
for Everyone

In the beginning, God created Adam and Eve so that they could live happily alongside Him in the Garden of Eden. But Adam and Eve decided to disobey God, and they ate from the forbidden tree.

God, who is just, had to remove them from the garden, and Adam and Eve became separated from God. Since then, people have always done wrong things, moving them further and further from God.

Even today, we all
do things God does not like.
No one is perfectly good.

But God
loves us so much
that He sent His Son Jesus to live with us.

Jesus paid for all the bad things we've done by dying on a cross. He was punished for you and me.

> Do you think any of your friends would agree to be punished for a bad thing that you did?

Jesus did! He went to the cross to die, even though He had done nothing wrong. But on the third day, He rose again, and now He lives forever.

God wants you to know that you do wrong things, called sins. We all sin. When we feel sorry for our sins, we can pray to God and ask Him to forgive us. And He will! He promises to forgive us because Jesus has saved us. And we can live forever with God too.

Jesus is your friend.

He is my friend too!

Jesus died to save everyone.

My Bright Prayer

Dear God,
Thank You for waking me every morning
and for being with me all night.
Thank You for the sun and moon
and twinkly stars so bright.

But most of all, thank You for Your LIGHT!
Jesus, the light of the world,
I open my heart for You.
Shine bright in my life.
Amen.

My Favorite Bible Story

286 (Draw a story you like.)

My Favorite Bible Character

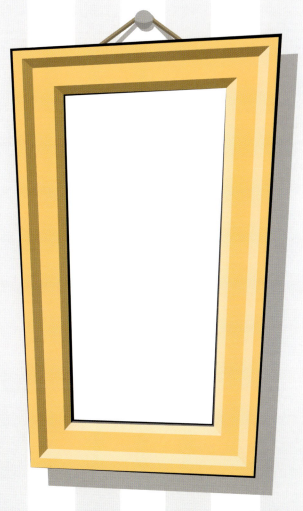

(Draw a Bible person you like.)